MW00909226

Nutrition
Exam Prep Guide

PEARSON
Prentice
Hall

Upper Saddle River, New Jersey
Columbus, Ohio

NATIONAL
RESTAURANT
ASSOCIATION
S O L U T I O N S ™

DISCLAIMER:

The information presented in this publication is provided for informational purposes only and is not intended to provide legal advice or establish standards of reasonable behavior. Customers who develop food safety-related or operational policies and procedures are urged to obtain the advice and guidance of legal counsel. Although **National Restaurant Association Solutions, LLC (NRA Solutions)** endeavors to include accurate and current information compiled from sources believed to be reliable, **NRA Solutions**, and its **licensor, the National Restaurant Association Educational Foundation (NRAEF)**, distributors, and agents make no representations or warranties as to the accuracy, currency, or completeness of the information. No responsibility is assumed or implied by the NRAEF, NRA Solutions, distributors, or agents for any damage or loss resulting from inaccuracies or omissions or any actions taken or not taken based on the content of this publication.

Sample questions are designed to familiarize the student with format, length and style of the examination questions, and represent only a sampling of topic coverage. The performance level on sample questions does not guarantee passing of a ManageFirst Program examination. Further, the distribution of sample exam questions with their focus on particular areas of subject matter within a ManageFirst Competency Guide is not necessarily reflective of how the questions will be distributed across subject matter on the actual correlating ManageFirst exam.

Visit www.restaurant.org for information on other National Restaurant Association Solutions products and programs.

ManageFirst Program™, ServSafe®, and ServSafe Alcohol® are registered trademarks or trademarks of the National Restaurant Association Educational Foundation, used under license by National Restaurant Association Solutions, LLC a wholly owned subsidary of the National Restaurant Association.

10 9 8 7 6 5 4 3
ISBN-13: 978-0-13-501896-5
ISBN-10:   0-13-501896-X

10 9 8 7 6 5 4 3 2 1

Contents

How to Take the ManageFirst Examination   1

Chapter Summaries and Objectives   9

Nutrition Practice Questions   21

Answer Key   33

Explanations to Answers   35

Glossary   49

How to Take the ManageFirst Examination

The ability to take tests effectively is a learned skill. There are specific things you can do to prepare yourself physically and mentally for an exam. This section helps you prepare and do your best on the ManageFirst Examination.

I. BEFORE THE EXAM

A. How to Study

Study the right material the right way. There is a lot of information and material in each course. How do you know what to study so you are prepared for the exam? This guide highlights what you need to know.

1. **Read the Introduction to each *Competency Guide*.** The beginning section of each guide explains the features and how it is organized.

2. **Look at how each chapter is organized and take clues from the book.**

    ■ *The text itself is important.* If the text is bold, large, or italicized you can be sure it is a key point that you should understand.

    ■ *The very first page tells you what you will learn.*

       Inside This Chapter: This tells you at a high level what will be covered in the chapter. Make sure you understand what each section covers. If you have studied the chapter but cannot explain what each section pertains to, you need to review that material.

Learning Objectives: After completing each chapter, you should be able to accomplish the specific goals and demonstrate what you have learned after reading the material. The practice exam as well as the actual exam questions relate to these learning objectives.

■ *Quizzes and Tests*

Test Your Knowledge: This is a pretest found at the beginning of each chapter to see how much you already know. Take this quiz to help you determine which areas you need to study and focus on.

■ *Key Terms* are listed at the beginning of each chapter and set in bold the first time they are referred to in the chapter. These terms—new and specific to the topic or ones you are already familiar with—are key to understanding the chapter's content. When reviewing the material, look for the key terms you don't know or understand and review the corresponding paragraph.

■ *Exhibits* visually depict key concepts and include charts, tables, photographs, and illustrations. As you review each chapter, find out how well you can explain the concepts illustrated in the exhibits.

■ *Additional Exercises*

Think About It sidebars are designed to provoke further thought and/or discussion and require understanding of the topics.

Activity boxes are designed to check your understanding of the material and help you apply your knowledge. The activities relate to a learning objective.

■ *Summary* reviews all the important concepts in the chapter and helps you retain and master the material.

3. **Attend Review Sessions or Study Groups**. Review sessions, if offered, cover material that will most likely be on the test. If separate review sessions are not offered, make sure you attend class the day before the exam. Usually, the instructor will review the material during this class. If you are a social learner, study with other students; discussing the topics with other students may help your comprehension and retention.

4. **Review the Practice Questions,** which are designed to help you prepare for the exam. Sample questions are designed to familiarize the student with the format, length, and style of the exam questions, and represent only a sampling of topic coverage on the final exam. The performance level on sample questions does not guarantee passing of a ManageFirst Program exam.

B. How to Prepare Physically and Mentally

Make sure you are ready to perform your best during the exam. Many students do everything wrong when preparing for an exam. They stay up all night, drink coffee to stay awake, or take sleep aids which leave them groggy and tired on test day.

There are practical things to do to be at your best. If you were an athlete preparing for a major event, what would you do to prepare yourself? You wouldn't want to compete after staying up all night or drinking lots of caffeine. The same holds true when competing with your brain!

1. **Get plenty of sleep.** Lack of sleep makes it difficult to focus and recall information. Some tips to help you get a good night's sleep are:

   - Make sure you have studied adequately enough days before the exam so that you do not need to cram and stay up late the night before the test.
   - Eat a good dinner the night before and a good breakfast the day of the exam.
   - Do not drink alcohol or highly-caffeinated drinks.
   - Exercise during the day, but not within four hours of bedtime.
   - Avoid taking sleep aids.

2. **Identify and control anxiety.** It is important to know the difference between actual test anxiety and anxiety caused by not being prepared.

Test anxiety is an actual physical reaction. If you know the information when you are **not** under pressure but feel physically sick and cannot recall information during the exam, you probably suffer from test anxiety. In this case, you may need to learn relaxation techniques or get some counseling. The key is how you react under pressure.

If you cannot recall information during reviews or the practice exam when you are not under pressure, you have not committed the information to memory and need to study more.

- Make sure you are as prepared as possible. (See "Anxiety Caused by Lack of Preparation")
- Take the exam with a positive attitude.
- Do not talk to other students who may be pessimistic or negative about the exam.
- Know what helps you relax and do it (chewing gum, doodling, breathing exercises).
- Make sure you understand the directions. Ask the instructor questions *before* the test begins.
- The instructor or proctor may only talk to you if you have defective materials or need to go to the restroom. They cannot discuss any questions.
- The instructor or proctor may continuously monitor the students so do not be nervous if they walk around the room.
- Know the skills described in Section II, During the Test.

3. **Anxiety Caused by Lack of Preparation.** The best way to control anxiety due to lack of preparation is focus on the exam. Whenever possible, you should know and do the following:

- Know the location of the exam and how to get there.
- Know if it is a paper-and-pencil test or an online exam. Pencils may be available but bring sufficient number 2 pencils if taking the paper-and-pencil version of the exam.
- If it is an online exam you may need your email address, if you have one, to receive results.
- You are prohibited from using purses, books, papers, pagers, cell phones, or other recording devices during the exam.
- Calculators and scratch paper may be used, if needed. Be sure your calculator is working properly and has fresh batteries.
- The exam is not a timed; however, it is usually completed in less than two hours.
- Take the sample exam so you know what format, style, and content to expect.
- Arrive early so you don't use valuable testing time to unpack.

II. DURING THE TEST

An intent of National Restaurant Association Solutions' ManageFirst exams is to make sure you have met certain learning objectives. If you are physically prepared, have studied the material, and taken the practice exam, you should find the ManageFirst exams to be very valid and fair. Remember, successful test taking is a skill. Understanding the different aspects of test preparation and exam taking will help ensure your best performance.

A. Test Taking Strategies

- Preview the exam for a quick overview of the length and questions.
- Do not leave any question unanswered.
- Answer the questions you are sure of first.

- Stop and check occasionally to make sure you are putting your answer in the correct place on the answer sheet. If you are taking an online exam, you will view one question at a time.
- Do not spend too much time on any one question. If you do not know the answer after reasonable consideration, move on and come back to it later.
- Make note of answers about which you are unsure so you can return to them.
- Review the exam at the end to check your answers and make sure all questions are answered.

B. Strategies for Answering Multiple-Choice Questions

Multiple-choice tests are objective. The correct answer is there, you just need to identify it.

- Try to answer the question before you look at the options.
- Use the process of elimination. Eliminate the answers you know are incorrect.
- Your first response is usually correct.

III. AFTER THE EXAM

Learn from each exam experience so you can do better on the next. If you did not perform on the exam as you expected, determine the reason. Was it due to lack of studying or preparation? Were you unable to control your test anxiety? Were you not focused enough because you were too tired? Identifying the reason allows you to spend more time on that aspect before your next exam. Use the information to improve on your next exam.

If you do not know the reason, you should schedule a meeting with the instructor. As all NRA Solutions ManageFirst exams are consistent, it is important to understand and improve your exam performance. If you cannot identify your problem areas, your errors will most likely be repeated on consecutive exams.

IV. EXAM DAY DETAILS

The information contained in this section will help ensure that you are able to take the exam on the scheduled test day and that you know what to expect and are comfortable about taking the exam.

- Have your photo identification available.
- Anyone with special needs must turn in an *Accommodation Request* to the instructor at least 10 days prior to the exam to receive approval and allow time for preparations. *If needs are not known 10 days prior, you may not be able to take the exam on the scheduled test day.*
- A bilingual English-native language dictionary may be used by anyone who speaks English as a second language. The dictionary will be inspected to make sure there are no notes or extra papers in it.
- If you are ill and must leave the room after the exam has begun you must turn in your materials to the instructor or proctor. If you are able to return, your materials will be returned to you and you may complete the exam. If it is an online exam you must close your browser and if the exam has not been graded yet, login in again when you return.
- Restroom breaks are allowed. Only one person may go at a time and all materials must be turned in prior to leaving the room and picked up when you return; or you must close your browser and login again for online exams.
- Make-up tests may be available if you are unable to take the exam on test day. Check with your instructor for details.
- If you are caught cheating you will not receive a score and must leave the exam location.

Nutrition
Chapter Summaries and Objectives

Chapter 1 Nutritional Cooking—Art and Science

Summary

Good nutrition is good for everyone. It leads to better health and stamina, and it leads to greater success in the restaurant and foodservice business. Restaurant and foodservice professionals educated in nutrition are needed to provide nutritious food for all modern dining situations. When you, as a professional, understand the dynamics of combining nutrition science and culinary art, you will be able to provide food that meets the needs of the consumer for nutrition and sensory enjoyment.

Although humanity has had thousands of years to develop nutritional needs and traditional ways to meet them, we have had only a few years of research to uncover the body's true nutritional needs and *better* ways to meet them. This knowledge continues to increase, resulting in progressive improvements in the principles of nutrition.

With a solid foundation of knowledge of nutrition, restaurant and foodservice professionals can develop or modify recipes and menus to give them more nutritional balance while maintaining the taste and other sensory appeals they have. Doing this involves a combination of cooking art and nutritional science.

After completing this chapter, you should be able to:
- Explain the importance of nutrition in the foodservice and restaurant industry.
- Explain why achieving balanced nutrition is important.
- Explain why making food both nutritious and interesting is important.
- Explain how principles of nutrition are dynamic and change as scientists learn more about food and metabolism.
- List the factors that affect people's food choices.

- Explain why restaurateurs are becoming more aware of the need to provide good nutrition in all menus.
- Explain how to obtain nutrition information for recipes and menus.
- Explain, in general, how making food both nutritious and interesting is a combination of art and science.

Chapter 2 The Basic Nutrients—Their Importance in Health

Summary

Nutrients are chemical substances that provide nourishment to the body. There are six basic classes of nutrients importance to the body that are found in food. They are: carbohydrates, proteins, lipids, vitamins, minerals, and water. In addition to the six basic classes of nutrients, there are phytonutrients, or phytochemicals, found in some food that help to prevent disease. Carbohydrate and protein provide four kilocalories of energy per gram, and lipid provides nine kilocalories of energy per gram. Although proteins can supply energy, they are not normally used this way but, instead, are used to provide building blocks in the form of amino acids. Alcohol is a non-nutrient that provides seven kilocalories of energy per gram. Digestion and absorption are complicated processes that separate nutrients and incorporate them into the body.

After completing this chapter, you should be able to:
- List the six basic types of nutrients found in food along with their characteristics.
- Describe the major functions of carbohydrates, proteins, and lipids in the body.
- Describe the roles of vitamins, minerals, and water.
- Explain the effect of alcohol consumption on the body.
- List reasons to decrease the consumption of empty-calorie food.
- Describe the digestion, absorption, and transport of nutrients.
- List the organs of digestive system and the major function of each.

Chapter 3 Understanding Nutritional Standards and Guidelines

Summaries

Healthful diets contain the amounts of essential nutrients and calories needed to prevent nutritional deficiencies and excesses. Healthful diets, along with physical activity, also provide the right balance of nutrients and healthy lifestyle habits to reduce risks of disease.

Dietary planning, whether for an individual or a group, involves offering menu choices that are nutritionally adequate, with the help of tools such as the Food Guide Pyramid. Food choices are the result of history, culture, and environment, as well as energy and nutrient needs. People also eat food for enjoyment. Family, friends, and beliefs play a major role in the way people select food and plan meals.

Many genetic, environmental, behavioral, and cultural factors can affect health. Understanding their own family histories of disease or risk factors can help consumers make informed food choices. Healthful diets help people o f all ages to have the energy they need to work productively and feel their best. Food choices also can help reduce the risk of disease.

After completing this chapter, you should be able to:
- Explain and use Dietary Reference Intakes, *Dietary Guidelines for Americans 2005,* MyPyramid, Daily Values, and food labels to assess the adequacy of a diet or set of menu choices.
- Use the USDA's MyPyramid to evaluate the food groups and portion sizes of a diet or set of menu choices.
- Assess the adequacy of portions in menu development.
- Describe food-labeling requirements.
- Summarize the Nutritional Labeling and Education Act of 1990 (NLEA) as it relates to restaurant and foodservice operations.
- State the FDA requirements for food to be labeled "healthy."

Chapter 4 Carbohydrates

Summary

Carbohydrates include sugars, starches, fiber, and oxygen and yield four kilocalories of energy per gram of food. They are abundant in pasta, rice, bread, tortillas, vegetables, fruit, and beans, among others. They fuel the body, spare protein for important purposes, and become part of the body's structure. The Dietary Reference Intakes provide a Recommended Dietary Allowance for intakes of carbohydrates and adequate intakes for fiber, which vary by a person's age, gender, and activity level. About half of a person's caloric intake should come from carbohydrates. If overall caloric intake is in line with bodily needs, eating carbohydrates will not cause weight gain.

Both type 1 and type 2 diabetes are increasing in the United Sates, the greatest change being the increased incidence of type 2, especially in children. In addition, medical professionals believe most of it may be preventable because it is the result of obesity.

After completing this chapter, you should be able to:
- Define the term carbohydrate.
- State the recommended dietary allowances (RDA) for carbohydrate.
- Name the types of carbohydrates in the diet.
- State the types of dietary fiber and their importance to health.
- List types of food that are good sources of dietary fiber.
- Explain how the body metabolizes and stores carbohydrate.
- Explain diabetes and its causes and effects.

Chapter 5 Proteins

Summary

Protein is made up of amino acids and has four kilocalories per gram. Protein is found in food like beef and chicken as well as in grains and vegetables; however, fruit is relatively low in protein. Vegetarians can obtain adequate amounts of protein from vegetable and grain sources, as long as all of the essential amino acids are consumed. Typically, vegetarians must consume complementary protein food items to do this.

Protein is an important macronutrient in people's diets that carries out numerous essential functions. However, consuming more protein than required by the body does not increase muscle mass or necessarily make you healthier.

The information in this chapter should serve as a foundation of knowledge regarding protein that will inform both your daily activities in the culinary world and your own dietary standards.

After completing this chapter, you should be able to:
- Describe the makeup and characteristics of protein.
- List the functions of protein in the body.
- Explain essential amino acids and complete proteins.
- Explain how complementary incomplete proteins combined can equal complete proteins.
- Explain the effects of excessive and insufficient protein intake.
- State the recommended protein intake for humans.
- List good sources of protein in the diet.

Chapter 6 Fats and Other Lipids

Summary

Fat is an essential nutrient to the human body. Tissue development, energy, and the body's ability to heal all depend on fatty acids found in food. When determining what food is best for the diet, people must pay more attention to the type of fat rather than the amount of fat found in the nutritional makeup of food items.

Lipids include triglycerides, cholesterol, and phospholipids. Whether found in plants, animals, or eggs, each of these types of fats must be stored, prepared, and consumed in ways that will not cause harm to the body. Linoleic and alpha-linolenic acid are to essential fatty acids found in polyunsaturated oils. These acids are necessary for normal growth and development. A deficiency in these may cause dermatitis, diarrhea, infections, and stunted growth and wound healing.

Rancidity is most common in unsaturated fats. Two general types of rancidity are hydrolytic and oxidative, which either yield water or react to air. Proper storage will prevent most fats from going rancid and losing flavor.

Lipoproteins are the combination of lipids and protein as they link together before passing cholesterol, triglycerides, and phospholipids to cells throughout the body. The density of these lipoproteins is based upon the amount of protein contained in the molecule. A lipoprotein molecule is created in the liver and intestines and travels through the body as a very low-density lipoprotein (VLDL), picking up cholesterol, phospholipids, and protein until it develops into a low density lipoprotein (LDL). LDL is often blocked by saturated fats that cause cholesterol levels to rise, whereas HDL can lower cholesterol levels.

The body is equipped to handle all types of fat and fat-like substances, but it is very easy to harm the body by following poor dietary practices. The Food and Nutrition Board does not recommend frequent consumption of products with saturated fats or trans fatty acids. The American Heart Association recommends that people follow a diet regulating the quantities of calories from fat. They also have indicated a limit on cholesterol intake of less than 300 milligrams per day. By following these and other recommended dietary practices, the body can remain healthy by consuming the right food more often.

After completing this chapter, you should be able to:
- Describe the types of lipids found in food and their characteristics.
- Define these terms: fatty acids, cholesterol, and triglyceride.
- Explain the difference between saturated, monounsaturated, and polyunsaturated fatty acids.
- Describe how trans fatty acids are produced and their effect on health.
- List the essential fatty acids and their food sources.
- State the daily requirement for fats.
- Describe the digestion and absorption of fats.
- Explain the role of fats, oils, and cholesterol in health and disease.
- Describe the omega-3 and omega-6 fatty acids and their effects on health.

Chapter 7 Vitamins, Minerals, and Water

Summary

Vitamins, minerals, and water are essential to the human diet. Each vitamin has one or more specific functions and can be obtained from specific food sources. Vitamins are classified as either water-soluble or fat-soluble vitamins. The fat-soluble vitamins are important for human health for many reasons: vitamin A facilitates vision, vitamin D is necessary for bone health, vitamin E acts as an antioxidant, and vitamin K helps to prevent blood clotting. Among the water-soluble vitamins, the B vitamins act primarily as coenzymes for energy metabolism, and vitamin C acts as an antioxidant in the body. Deficiencies and toxicities of vitamins are possible, and some are serious.

The word "mineral" refers to chemical elements in the diet. Several elements are necessary for a variety of functions, and a deficiency in needed mineral results in a deficiency disease. Deficiencies of the minerals potassium, calcium, and magnesium may contribute to the incidence of high blood pressure. Calcium is well recognized for its role in healthy bones and teeth. Iron, zinc, and copper are important minerals that form hemoglobin.

There are established intake levels for vitamins and minerals, and obtaining too much can be a problem. Supplementation of vitamins and minerals may be warranted for specific people to avoid deficiencies, and some people choose to take a multivitamin each day to ensure receiving all of the needed vitamins and minerals. However, it is best to obtain vitamins and minerals from food sources because of the added benefits from fiber and phytochemicals in food. There are ways to minimize vitamin and mineral losses when cooking.

Water, the most important nutrient in the body, has several important functions that are necessary for health. The average-sized adult should have sixty-four ounces of water each day from food and liquids combined. Consuming a variety of food items from all of the food groups helps attain the recommended dietary allowance for vitamins, minerals, and water in your diet.

After completing this chapter, you should be able to:
- List the functions of vitamins, minerals, and water in the body.
- Distinguish between fat-soluble and water-soluble vitamins.
- State good food sources for specific vitamins and minerals.
- List vitamin- and mineral-deficiency diseases.
- List ways to retain the vitamin and mineral content of food while cooking.
- State when it is appropriate to supplement vitamins and minerals.

Chapter 8 Food with Nutritional Appeal

Summary

Consumers and food professionals are increasingly concerned with what goes into their food. Often their concerns have to do with how the food products are grown or harvested. They also relate to decisions made by restaurant and foodservice professionals such as sources of supply, types of food use, condition when received, and on-site storage and processing of food products.

Serving organic and local food products, buying seasonally, and if fresh is unavailable, using processed produce are ways to purchase food with good nutrition. Once in house, food should be stored under the appropriate conditions, prepared just before service, and cooked quickly with minimal holding to ensure nutritional quality.

Each point in the food system—growing, harvesting, processing, receiving, storing, preparing, and cooking—leaves the restaurant and foodservice professional with an opportunity to preserve the nutritional quality of the food at hand or cause it to deteriorate. Exposure to the air and to high temperatures and natural decaying processes cause deterioration of the nutrients in food products. Minimizing all these factors is necessary for food products to arrive at the stove or table with the maximum amount of nutrients.

After completing this chapter, you should be able to:
- Explain how the steps in the food-processing system affect nutritional content.
- Distinguish between organic, certified organic, natural, local, and conventional produce.
- Define genetically modified and bioengineered food products.
- List and explain processing and cooking techniques that can help to retain nutrients in food.

Chapter 9 Cooking and Eating More Healthfully

Summary

As a restaurant or foodservice professional, you can employ many techniques to improve the healthfulness of meals you serve. Substituting cooking methods, selecting healthy ingredients, adding healthy ingredients, and reducing levels of unhealthy ingredients are all techniques that will make a dish healthier.

When modifying food for nutrition, it is important to remember that the food needs to taste good and be attractively presented. When making specific substitutions, consider the function of the ingredient in the food and make the substitution accordingly. Incorporate healthy food with high flavor impact.

After completing this chapter, you should be able to:
- Explain techniques that can boost the flavor of food in a healthy way.
- Explain the importance of food's sensory appeal in promoting healthy eating.
- List and describe techniques for food preparation that preserve nutrients.
- Describe how common food preparations may be modified for improved nutrition.
- Explain techniques to lower the fat content of food.

Chapter 10 Eating in the United States

Summary

A healthy American diet has adequate carbohydrate, protein, and fat in the correct proportions for the level of activity the body receives, contains few empty calories, and has variety to ensure the proper intake of vitamins and minerals. However, the majority of Americans do not follow a healthy diet. Many factors, including large portion sizes and poor food choices, contribute to less-than-ideal diets.

A variety of diets are found in the United States. Some people adhere to special diets for philosophical, health, or religious reasons. For example, people following a vegetarian diet do not eat meat, fish, or fowl or products containing these items. Religion-influenced diets such as those followed by Jewish or Hindu people, restrict various food items and may restrict the way food is prepared and served.

There are also a number of fad diets. Fad diets often offer quick fixes and contradict recommendations made by reputable health organizations. For example, low-carbohydrate, high-fat, and high-protein diets are not balanced diets and may lack essential nutrients. The long-term effects of these diets are not known.

Major causes of disease and death in the United States are related to poor diet and a sedentary lifestyle. These conditions include cardiovascular disease, hypertension, type 2 diabetes, obesity, osteoporosis, iron-deficiency anemia, oral disease, malnutrition, and some cancers. The health problem most able to be overcome by an improved diet in the United States is overweight and obesity. Not only is adult obesity a problem, but teen and childhood obesity is growing at an alarming rate. Too many calories combined with a sedentary lifestyle is the main cause of obesity in the United States. Restaurant and foodservice operations can help by providing healthy, nutritious food that is low in excess fat, sugar, and other empty calories, and by providing sufficient choices for their customers.

Food items provide an array of nutrients that may have beneficial effects on health. However, for people with food allergies, some food items must be avoided. Although there are more than 160 food items that have been identified to cause food allergies in sensitive people, eight major allergens have been identified – milk and dairy products, eggs and egg products, fish, shellfish, tree nuts, peanuts, wheat, and soy and soy products. Restaurant and foodservice operations are responsible for ensuring that all servers, chefs, and kitchen staff are able to answer customers' questions about food allergens in the food they serve. In addition, restaurant and foodservice professionals have a responsibility to manage their menus so guests can make informed dining choices that help them maintain a balanced diet over a period of time.

After completing this chapter, you should be able to:
- Describe a healthy diet.
- Define the various types of vegetarian diets.
- Characterize diets related to ethnic/cultural, religious, and philosophical positions.
- Describe the nature and effects of various diets found in the United States.
- Describe sports diets and popular fad diets and their effects on the body.
- Characterize the impact and role of food additives and supplements in diets.
- Explain how to deal with allergens in food items.

Nutrition
Practice Questions

Please note the numbers in parentheses following each question. They represent the chapter and page number, respectively, where the content in found in the ManageFirst Competency Guide.

IMPORTANT: These sample questions are designed to familiarize the student with format, length and style of the examination questions, and represent only a sampling of topic coverage.

The grid below represents how the *actual* exam questions will be divided across content areas on the corresponding ManageFirst Program exam.

Nutrition			
	1.	Nutritional Cooking—Art and Science	13
	2.	The Basic Nutrients—Their Importance in Health	9
	3.	Understanding Nutritional Standards and Guidelines	8
	4.	Carbohydrates	6
	5.	Proteins	5
	6.	Fats and Other Lipids	6
	7.	Vitamins, Minerals, and Water	6
	8.	Food with Nutritional Appeal	10
	9.	Cooking and Eating More Healthfully	11
	10.	Eating in the United States	11
		Total No. of Questions	**85**

The performance level on sample questions does not guarantee passing of a ManageFirst Program examination. Further, the distribution of sample exam questions with their focus on particular areas of subject matter within a ManageFirst Competency Guide is not necessarily reflective of how the questions will be distributed across subject matter on the actual correlating ManageFirst exam.

1. What must carbohydrates be broken down into because only these are absorbed by the small intestines? (4, 70)
   A. Monosaccharides
   B. Disaccharides
   C. Polysaccharides
   D. Oligosaccharides

2. What are powerful muscles called that only allow food to pass in one direction under normal circumstances? (2, 29)
   A. Mucosa
   B. Sphincters
   C. Peristalsis
   D. Villi

3. What is a kilocalorie? (2, 23)
   A. A type of carbohydrate
   B. Made of carbon and water
   C. The same as a kilogram
   D. A unit of measurement for energy

4. What reduces cholesterol by dissolving in water and connecting to bile salts? (4, 73)
   A. Soluble fiber
   B. Complex carbohydrates
   C. Insoluble fiber
   D. Amino acids

5. How is peristalsis defined? (2, 28)
   A. Process of breaking down food into its most elemental parts
   B. Mechanical digestion of food by grinding and mixing food
   C. Fingerlike projections in the small intestine that increase surface area and absorptive capacity
   D. Involuntary wave of contraction that moves food through the digestive tract

6. A chef should strive to provide guests with tasty, nutritious foods that are lower in what? (9, 163)
   A. Complex carbohydrates
   B. Fat and salt
   C. Amino acids
   D. Omega-3 fatty acids

7. What is the membrane that protects the lining of the digestive tract and provides secretions from underlying tissue called? (2, 28)
   A. Mucosa
   B. Serosa
   C. Pancreas
   D. Submucosa

8. What taste helps keep people from eating poisonous foods? (9, 165)
   A. Sour
   B. Umami
   C. Bitter
   D. Salty

9. MyPyramid can be used by foodservice professionals to do what? (3, 48)
   A. Provide a more balanced menu
   B. Identify potential allergens in menu items
   C. Label menu items as heart healthy
   D. Meet the Food and Drug Administration's regulations

10. What is the definition of food science? (1, 15)
   A. Understanding of the function of food ingredients and the aesthetic profiles of food
   B. Study of changes that occur in food with chemical and physical reactions
   C. Application of technology to living organisms to produce something of use
   D. Study of nutrients in food and how they are ingested, digested, absorbed, transported, and used to maintain the body

11. Why is it important for foodservice operations to offer nutritious menu options? (1, 2)
    A. Consumers today are more concerned about their own nutrition.
    B. Creating nutritious menu options creates new jobs for nutritionists.
    C. Nutritious meals are cheaper for a foodservice operation to produce.
    D. Foodservice operations are obligated to make the consumer eat more nutritious food.

12. According to the Competency Guide, when modifying a recipe to reduce fat, what is it of the utmost importance to consider? (9, 176)
    A. Cost
    B. Portion size
    C. Salt content
    D. Taste

13. When does a body use protein as an energy source? (5, 87)
    A. When the body has extra protein available
    B. All the time; it is the major source of energy
    C. When a person is in a physical state of starvation
    D. After a high protein meal has been consumed

14. What does the process of partial hydrogenation create? (6, 108)
    A. Cholesterol
    B. Rancidity
    C. Linoleic acid
    D. Trans fats

15. What is the term often used to refer to chemicals that may help the body fight off disease? (2, 23)
    A. Lipoprotein
    B. Phytochemical
    C. Kilocalorie
    D. Organic

16. What is the primary reason people choose the foods they eat? (1, 7)
    A. Nutritional needs
    B. Advertisements
    C. Body weight
    D. Likes and dislikes

17. What does the width of the color bands on the MyPyramid symbol represent? (3, 44)
    A. Proportionality
    B. Variety
    C. Personalization
    D. Activity

18. What helps glucose enter cells and reduces blood-sugar levels? (4, 77)
    A. Glucagon
    B. Phytochemicals
    C. Insulin
    D. Glycogen

19. What are factors that influence nutritional needs? (2, 21)
    A. Age and ethnicity
    B. Body size and religion
    C. Gender and ethnicity
    D. Age and gender

20. What is used to produce genetically modified organisms? (8, 150)
    A. Irradiation
    B. Recombinant DNA technology
    C. Crossbreeding
    D. Selective breeding

21. Why might vegans suffer from diseases caused by vitamin deficiencies? (10, 193)
    A. They eat too many whole grains.
    B. Their diet excludes many food types.
    C. They include dairy products in their diet.
    D. Food items that meet vegan's requirements are scarce.

22. A carbohydrate is an organic compound that contains what? (4, 67)
    A. Carbon, nitrogen, and oxygen
    B. Hydrogen and sodium
    C. Carbon, hydrogen, and oxygen
    D. Carbon and nitrogen

23. Fats are _____ at room temperature. (6, 107)
    A. solid
    B. liquid
    C. saturated
    D. unsaturated

24. What is nutrient loss due to freezing an example of? (8, 152)
    A. Chemical loss
    B. Physical loss
    C. Harvest loss
    D. Irradiation loss

25. What is linoleic acid, an essential fatty acid, found in? (6, 110)
    A. Soybeans
    B. Milk
    C. Flaxseed
    D. Oranges

26. What vitamin is water-soluble? (7, 124)
    A. Vitamin A
    B. Vitamin E
    C. Vitamin K
    D. Vitamin C

27. Which of the following statements about temperature and the perception of saltiness is true? (9, 165)
    A. The hotter the food, the more salt is tasted.
    B. The hotter the food, the less salt is tasted.
    C. The colder the food, the less salt is tasted.
    D. Temperature has no affect on how salty food tastes.

28. What does the Food Allergen Labeling and Consumer Protection Act of 2004 apply to? (10, 210)
  A. All packaged products
  B. All unpackaged food products
  C. Domestically packaged food products only
  D. Packaged, FDA-regulated food items only

29. What is the process of breaking down food into elemental parts that can be absorbed and used by the body? (2, 28)
  A. Metabolism
  B. Digestion
  C. Nutrition
  D. Bioengineering

30. What are maltose and sucrose both examples of? (4, 70)
  A. Monosaccharides
  B. Disaccharides
  C. Polysaccharides
  D. Oligosaccharides

31. A person with a food allergy to peanuts (10, 211)
  A. is able eat foods fried in peanut oil.
  B. may eat small amounts of the food that contains peanuts.
  C. can eat foods that have touched peanuts but don't contain peanuts.
  D. must avoid any food that has come into contact with peanuts or contains peanuts.

32. What must a chef have a good understanding of in order to provide customers with tasty, low-fat, low-salt food? (9, 163)
  A. The latest fad diets
  B. The cost of ingredients
  C. Organic food items
  D. Healthful cooking techniques

33. What is a slow cooking method good for cooking tough, whole cuts of meat? (8, 156)
    A. Broiling
    B. Baking
    C. Braising
    D. Stewing

34. What is the part of the food label that contains FDA required nutrition information? (3, 52)
    A. Ingredient label
    B. Health claim
    C. Potential Allergen list
    D. Nutritional Facts panel

35. What are fats stored in the body as? (6, 106)
    A. Fatty acids
    B. Triglycerides
    C. Glucose
    D. Trans fat

36. Why do many fast food operations now offer items such as fruit cups as side dishes to their consumers? (1, 10)
    A. Consumers have a desire to eat quickly.
    B. Operations need to offer lower cost foods.
    C. Consumers are demanding healthy alternatives.
    D. The public has little interest in nutrition.

37. One way to make a recipe healthier is to replace ingredients. What should be considered first when replacing ingredients? (9, 172)
    A. Color
    B. Cost
    C. Availability
    D. Function

38. Why are proteins needed on a daily basis at every stage of life? (5, 87)
   A. They are the primary source of energy for the body.
   B. They are the predominant source of vitamins A and C.
   C. They support the growth and maintenance of cells.
   D. They contain the most essential fatty acids.

39. What is a vitamin that activates other enzymes called? (7, 123)
   A. Micronutrient
   B. Antioxidant
   C. Phytochemical
   D. Coenzyme

40. The Nutrition Facts panel provides the percentage of the Daily Value of a nutrient in a single serving of a food based on a _____ calorie diet. (3, 54)
   A. 1,200
   B. 1,600
   C. 2,000
   D. 2,400

41. What is the morbidity rate? (10, 204)
   A. Death rate in a population
   B. Obesity rate in a population
   C. Disease rate in a population
   D. Malnutrition rate in a population

42. A local restaurant wants to include more whole grains in its offerings. What dish could be added to the menu to help achieve this goal? (4, 74)
   A. Barley pilaf
   B. Spaghetti and meatballs
   C. Baked potatoes
   D. Blueberry pie

43. According to the Competency Guide, what must the Muslim diet exclude? (10, 196)
   A. Beef
   B. Pork
   C. Chicken
   D. Fish

44. What type of cooking method prepares meat on a grate over heat that may be direct or indirect? (9, 174)
   A. Grilling
   B. Braising
   C. Poaching
   D. Roasting

45. According to the Competency Guide, what is usually true of the items carrying the label "low carbohydrate?" (10, 199)
   A. The food is low in carbohydrates and healthier.
   B. The food is low in carbohydrates and calories.
   C. The food meets FDA guidelines regulating low carbohydrate foods.
   D. There are no legal guidelines defining low carbohydrate, so it means very little.

46. What process does a protein go through when it is heated? (5, 94)
   A. Decomposition
   B. Denaturation
   C. Oxidative rancidity
   D. Flavor reversion

47. What are fad diets often based on? (10, 197)
   A. A limited understanding of nutrition
   B. Solid nutritional research and knowledge
   C. FDA guidelines for a nutritious diet
   D. The MyPyramid food categories and proportions

48. What was invented when cooking techniques improved and food began to be prepared for sensory enjoyment as well as survival? (1, 6)
   A. Culinary arts
   B. Food science
   C. Meat preservation
   D. Nutritional cooking

49. What does the "Certified Organic" label on a jar of fruit juice indicate about the juice? (8, 149)
   A. Meets the requirements of a certifying agency
   B. Has been grown on a small co-operative farm
   C. Has more nutrients than conventionally produced juice
   D. Meets universally accepted organic food standards

50. To help ensure that consumers are getting safe food, how is conventional food grown? (8, 149)
   A. Using organic, pesticide-free farming methods
   B. Using any pesticide, fertilizer, or hormone available
   C. With only pesticides and fertilizers labeled natural
   D. With fertilizers, pesticides, hormones, and drugs recognized as safe

Nutrition
Answer Key to Practice Questions

1. A	26.D
2. B	27.B
3. D	28.D
4. A	29.B
5. D	30.B
6. B	31.D
7. A	32.D
8. C	33.C
9. A	34.D
10.B	35.B
11.A	36.C
12.D	37.D
13 C	38.C
14.D	39.D
15.B	40.C
16.D	41.C
17.A	42.A
18.C	43.B
19.D	44.A
20.B	45.D
21.B	46.B
22.C	47.A
23.A	48.A
24.A	49.A
25.A	50.D

Nutrition
Explanations to the Answers for the Practice Questions

Question #1

Answer A is correct. Only monosaccharides, a molecule consisting of a single sugar unit, can cross the intestinal cells of the small intestine.

Answer B is wrong. Disaccharides are double-sugars and must be broken down.

Answer C is wrong. Polysaccharides consist of twenty to thousands of sugar units and must be broken down.

Answer D is wrong. Oligosaccharides have three to ten sugar molecules and must be broken down.

Question #2

Answer A is wrong. Mucosa is a mucous membrane lining the digestive tract.

Answer B is correct. Sphincters are muscles that close after food has been passed on to the next level of digestion.

Answer C is wrong. Peristalsis is an involuntary wave of contractions that move the food through the digestive tract.

Answer D is wrong. Villi are fingerlike projections in the small intestines that absorb nutrients.

Question #3

Answer A is wrong. A carbohydrate is a class of nutrients, not a unit of measure.

Answer B is wrong. A kilocalorie is a unit of measure. It is not *made* of anything.

Answer C is wrong. A kilogram is a unit of measure, but it measures weight.

Answer D is correct. A kilocalorie is a unit of measurement for energy that equals one thousand calories.

Question #4

Answer A is correct. Soluble fiber dissolves in water to form a gel that connects to bile salts and reduces cholesterol.

Answer B is wrong. Complex carbohydrates are chains of sugars and do not reduce cholesterol.

Answer C is wrong. Insoluble fiber does not dissolve in water.

Answer D is wrong. Amino acids are organic molecules that make up proteins.

Question #5

Answer A is wrong. This process is digestion.

Answer B is wrong. This process is mastication.

Answer C is wrong. The fingerlike projections in the small intestine are villi.

Answer D is correct. Peristalsis is an involuntary wave of contraction that moves food through the digestive tract.

Question #6

Answer A is wrong. Complex carbohydrates come from wholesome foods such as legumes and vegetables. This type of carbohydrate is more desirable than simple sugars.

Answer B is correct. Lowering salt and fat in foods while retaining taste should be a chef's goal.

Answer C is wrong. Amino acids make up proteins and are an essential part of any diet.

Answer D is wrong. Omega-3 fatty acids are required by the body and need to be included in the diet each day.

Question # 7

Answer A is correct. The mucous membrane protecting the lining of the digestive tract is called the mucosa.

Answer B is wrong. The serosa lines the abdominal cavity.

Answer C is wrong. The pancreas is an organ.

Answer D is wrong. The submucosa is connective tissue that supports the mucosa.

Question # 8
Answer A is wrong. Sour taste is a sharp sensation found in citrus, vinegars, etc. It is not a warning sensation.
Answer B is wrong. Umami has been recently recognized as the fifth taste sensation. It is the savory taste and can enhance other flavors.
Answer C is correct. Poisonous alkaloidal food is most associated with the bitter taste.
Answer D is wrong. The salty taste enhances flavor. People can condition their preference for salt to high or low amounts but the presence of this taste does not indicate poison.

Question #9
Answer A is correct. The MyPyramid can be used as a guide to what constitutes a healthful diet and to help plan more balanced menus.
Answer B is wrong. Food labels are used to identify ingredients that are potential allergens.
Answer C is wrong. The FDA regulates labels such as "heart healthy" by requiring an operation to provide a reasonable basis for the claim.
Answer D is wrong. MyPyramid is a tool developed by the USDA for educational purposes, not to regulate menus or foodservice operations.

Question #10
Answer A is wrong. This is the art of cooking.
Answer B is correct. The study of chemical and physical reactions that occur in food is called food science.
Answer C is wrong. This is biotechnology, also known as bioengineering.
Answer D is wrong. This is nutrition.

Question #11
Answer A is correct. Many customers today are more aware and concerned about their nutritional needs and foodservice operations must strive to meet the customer's demands.
Answer B is wrong. This may be a side-effect of creating more nutritious menus, but it is not the objective.
Answer C is wrong. Cost may be increased by offering more nutritious options.
Answer D is wrong. A foodservice operation can't make a consumer eat a more healthy diet.

Question #12
Answer A is wrong. The goal is to cut fat, not cost. Cost is often a concern in menu planning but, in this case, it is not an important factor in the modification.
Answer B is wrong. Portion size can be used to reduce fat, but it does not involve recipe modification.
Answer C is wrong. The goal is to cut fat, not salt.
Answer D is correct. When modifying recipes it is of the utmost importance that the modified recipe taste good.

Question #13
Answer A is wrong. Carbohydrates and fats are the preferred sources of energy. Protein is only used as an energy source when a person is in a physical state of starvation or the body has depleted its source of carbohydrates and fats.
Answer B is wrong. See the explanation for answer A.
Answer C is correct. See the explanation for answer A.
Answer D is wrong. See the explanation for answer A.

Question #14
Answer A is wrong. Cholesterol is a naturally occurring lipid found in animal products.
Answer B is wrong. Rancidity occurs when fats and oils deteriorate.
Answer C is wrong. Linoleic acid is a naturally occurring essential fatty acid.
Answer D is correct. Trans fats are formed when oils have been partially hydrogenated. This process involves chemical reactions with hydrogen to make oils more solid and to increase shelf life.

Question #15
Answer A is wrong. A lipoprotein is a molecule combining a lipid and a protein.
Answer B is correct. A phytochemical is any chemical or nutrient derived from a plant, but the term is also commonly used to refer to chemicals that somehow aid the body in fighting and avoiding disease.
Answer C is wrong. A kilocalorie is a measurement of energy.
Answer D is wrong. Organic is a food label that means the product meets certain USDA requirements in the growing and production of the food.

Question #16
Answer A is wrong. Nutritional needs are a distant second to taste (likes and dislikes).
Answer B is wrong. Advertisements influence food choices, but the primary reason for choosing a food is taste (likes and dislikes).
Answer C is wrong. Body weight is influenced by food choices not the other way around.
Answer D is correct. Likes and dislikes are the primary reasons for making food choices.

Question #17
Answer A is correct. The width of each colored band on the pyramid suggests how much food a person should choose from each food group. The wider the band, the more of that type of food that should be eaten.
Answer B is wrong. Variety is represented by the different colors of the bands.
Answer C is wrong. The person on the steps represents personalization.
Answer D is wrong. The steps and the person climbing the steps represent activity level.

Question #18
Answer A is wrong. Glucagon is a hormone that counteracts insulin and raises low blood sugar.
Answer B is wrong. Phytochemicals help fight diseases but do not control blood-sugar levels.
Answer C is correct. Insulin is a hormone that helps glucose enter the cell, thus reducing blood-sugar levels.
Answer D is wrong. Glycogen is the form in which the body stores carbohydrates.

Question #19
Answer A is wrong. Ethnicity is does not influence nutritional needs.
Answer B is wrong. Religion does not influence nutritional needs.
Answer C is wrong. Ethnicity is does not influence nutritional needs.
Answer D is correct. Age and gender are two of the factors that influence nutritional needs.

Question #20
Answer A is wrong. Irradiation is used to reduce or eliminate bacteria and parasites that can cause foodborne illnesses.
Answer B is correct. Genetically modified organisms are plants or animals whose genetic makeup has been altered using recombinant DNA technology.
Answer C is wrong. Crossbreeding is the breeding of different varieties of plants or animals that have the best qualities of each species.
Answer D is wrong. Selective breeding is when the best plants of a harvest or the best animals of a herd are selected for reproduction.

Question #21
Answer A is wrong. Eating whole grains is healthy and nutritious.
Answer B is correct. Vegans eat no animal products, so they must be very careful avoid vitamin deficiencies and their accompanying diseases by eating supplemented foods or taking supplements.
Answer C is wrong. Vegans eat no dairy products.
Answer D is wrong. In addition to specialty stores that cater to vegetarians and vegans, many restaurants and chain grocery stores now carry items that meet their dietary requirements.

Question #22
Answer A is wrong. Carbohydrates do not contain nitrogen.
Answer B is wrong. Carbohydrates do not contain sodium.
Answer C is correct. Carbohydrates are made up of carbon, hydrogen, and oxygen.
Answer D is wrong. Carbohydrates do not contain nitrogen.

Question #23
Answer A is correct. Fats are triglycerides derived from animal sources that are solid at room temperature.
Answer B is wrong. Oils are triglycerides derived from plant sources that are liquid at room temperature.
Answer C is wrong. Saturated refers to the absence of double bonds between carbon atoms in the carbon chain.
Answer D is wrong. Unsaturated refers to the presence of one or more double bonds between carbon atoms in a carbon chain.

Question #24
Answer A is correct. Freezing causes nutrient loss due to a change in chemical composition of a food.
Answer B is wrong. Physical loss is caused by removal of part of the food.
Answer C is wrong. There is no actual term called harvest loss; however, loss during harvest would be physical.
Answer D is wrong. Irradiation of food does not cause loss of nutrients.

Question #25
Answer A is correct. Soybeans contain linoleic acid.
Answer B is wrong. Milk does not contain linoleic acid.
Answer C is wrong. Flaxseed is a source of alpha-linolenic acid.
Answer D is wrong. Oranges do not contain linoleic acid.

Question #26
Answer A is wrong. Vitamin A is a fat-soluble vitamin.
Answer B is wrong. Vitamin E is a fat-soluble vitamin.
Answer C is wrong. Vitamin K is a fat-soluble vitamin.
Answer D is correct. Vitamin C is a water-soluble vitamin.

Question #27
Answer A is wrong. The hotter the food, the less salt is tasted. The salty taste becomes more predominant as it cools.
Answer B is correct. See the explanation for answer A.
Answer C is wrong. See the explanation for answer A.
Answer D is wrong. See the explanation for answer A.

Question #28
Answer A is wrong. The FALCPA only applies to domestic and imported packaged food items that are subject to FDA regulations.
Answer B is wrong. The FALCPA only applies to packaged food products.
Answer C is wrong. See the explanation for answer A.
Answer D is correct. See the explanation for answer A.

Question #29

Answer A is wrong. Metabolism is the process by which the body converts the food into energy.

Answer B is correct. Digestion is the process of breaking down food into elemental parts that can be absorbed and used by the body.

Answer C is wrong. Nutrition is the science of nutrients in food and how they are ingested, digested, absorbed, transported, and utilized by the body.

Answer D is wrong. Bioengineering is the application of technology to living organisms to produce something of use.

Question #30

Answer A is wrong. Fructose, glucose, and galactose are monosaccharides.

Answer B is correct. Maltose and sucrose are disaccharides, as is lactose.

Answer C is wrong. A polysaccharide is a long chain of glucose bonded together as a starch.

Answer D is wrong. Oligosaccharides are smaller complex carbohydrates. An example of an oligosaccharide is raffinose.

Question # 31

Answer A is wrong. A person with a food allergy must avoid the food completely, including oils made from the allergenic food and any food that has come into contact with the allergenic food.

Answer B is wrong. See the explanation for answer A.

Answer C is wrong. See the explanation for answer A.

Answer D is correct. See the explanation for answer A.

Question #32

Answer A is wrong. Fad diets are often not nutritionally sound, and they are not necessarily low fat or low salt.

Answer B is wrong. Ingredient cost is not relevant to preparing tasty, low-fat, low-salt food.

Answer C is wrong. Organic foods do not have to be used in preparing tasty, low-fat, low-salt food.

Answer D is correct. The chef in an operation must have a good understanding of healthful cooking techniques to provide customers with tasty food that is lower in fat and salt.

Question #33
Answer A is wrong. Broiling should be used for tender cuts of meat.
Answer B is wrong. Baking does not refer to cooking meat.
Answer C is correct. Braising is a slow, flavorful method of cooking used with tough cuts of meat. In this method, the whole food item is used.
Answer D is wrong. Stewing is similar to braising, but the meat is cut into pieces.

Question #34
Answer A is wrong. The ingredients are listed in a separate area of the label.
Answer B is wrong. Health claims are often made on labels but are not part of the FDA required nutrition information.
Answer C is wrong. Major allergens must be listed according to the FALCPA, but this is not part of the FDA-required nutrition information.
Answer D is correct. The Nutrition Facts panel contains the nutrition information required by the FDA.

Question #35
Answer A is wrong. Fatty acids bond with glycerol to form a triglyceride molecule.
Answer B is correct. Triglycerides are the form in which fats are stored in the body.
Answer C is wrong. Glucose is a carbohydrate.
Answer D is wrong. A trans fat is a partially hydrogenated oil.

Question #36
Answer A is wrong. Fast food has always catered to the consumer's desire to eat quickly.
Answer B is wrong. A fruit cup isn't necessarily less expensive than a less-healthy side dish.
Answer C is correct. Consumers want the convenience of eating quickly while having healthier alternatives offered to them by quick service operations.
Answer D is wrong. Consumers are increasingly concerned with nutrition.

Question #37
Answer A is wrong. The first consideration should be the function of the ingredient. If the replacement does not function properly as a replacement, then none of the other considerations matter. For example, egg whites give structure and their replacement must fulfill this function or the recipe will not work.
Answer B is wrong. See the explanation for answer A.
Answer C is wrong. See the explanation for answer A.
Answer D is correct. See the explanation for answer A.

Question #38
Answer A is wrong. Fats and carbohydrates are the best sources of energy for the body.
Answer B is wrong. Vitamins A and D are found in vegetables and fruits, which are carbohydrates.
Answer C is correct. Amino acids, the building blocks of protein, are needed daily for cell and tissue growth and maintenance.
Answer D is wrong. Essential fatty acids are lipids, not proteins.

Question #39
Answer A is wrong. All vitamins are micronutrients, but not all of them activate enzymes.
Answer B is wrong. An antioxidant is a vitamin that fights the excessive oxidation of molecules in the body.
Answer C is wrong. Phytochemicals are not nutrients and they are not required by the body, but they are thought to help fight disease.
Answer D is correct. Some vitamins act as coenzymes because they are activators of other enzymes.

Question #40
Answer A is wrong. The percentage of Daily Value is based on a 2,000-calorie diet.
Answer B is wrong. See the explanation for answer A.
Answer C is correct. See the explanation for answer A.
Answer D is wrong. See the explanation for answer A.

Question #41
Answer A is wrong. The death rate is called the mortality rate.
Answer B is wrong. The rate of obesity is not called the morbidity rate, although obesity might be considered a disease and counted in the morbidity rate.
Answer C is correct. The disease rate is also called the morbidity rate.
Answer D is wrong. Malnutrition is a disease that would be included in the morbidity rate.

Question # 42
Answer A is correct. Barley is a whole grain.
Answer B is wrong. Traditionally, spaghetti is made with processed flour with no whole grains.
Answer C is wrong. Baked potatoes are a starch, not a whole grain.
Answer D is wrong. Traditionally, pie is made with processed flour with no whole grains. Blueberries are not a grain.

Question #43
Answer A is wrong. Muslims can eat beef if it is slaughtered correctly.
Answer B is correct. Muslims can't eat any part of a pig.
Answer C is wrong. Correctly slaughtered chicken may be consumed.
Answer D is wrong. Muslims can eat fish.

Question #44
Answer A is correct. Grilling is the process of cooking food on a grate over direct or indirect heat.
Answer B is wrong. Braising is a slow cooking method in which the meat is half-submerged in liquid, covered, and allowed to cook gently for a long time.
Answer C is wrong. Poached meat or fish is gently cooked in liquid.
Answer D is wrong. Meat is roasted in a pan in an oven.

Question #45

Answer A is wrong. Low carbohydrate foods may be high in fats, salt, and calories.

Answer B is wrong. The food may be high in calories.

Answer C is wrong. There are no FDA guidelines.

Answer D is correct. There are no laws or guidelines regulating the use of the term "low carbohydrate."

Question #46

Answer A is wrong. Decomposition is the breaking down of an organism after death.

Answer B is correct. Denaturation is the unfolding of the protein's structure. This happens when heat is applied to a protein.

Answer C is wrong. This occurs when oils are exposed to air and heat.

Answer D is wrong. This is a slight oxidation of a fat before rancidity is apparent.

Question #47

Answer A is correct. Fad diets are based on a limited understanding of nutrition, body processes, and uses of food.

Answer B is wrong. A fad diet often goes against research and guidelines.

Answer C is wrong. See the explanation for answer B.

Answer D is wrong. See the explanation for answer B.

Question #48

Answer A is correct. Culinary arts was invented when cooking techniques improved and people became interested in taste.

Answer B is wrong. Food science is the study of food.

Answer C is wrong. Food preservation was invented long before culinary arts.

Answer D is wrong. Food enjoyment predates the understanding of nutrition.

Question #49

Answer A is correct. Certified organic food products meet the requirements of a certifying agency, such as a government agency or an independent organization.

Answer B is wrong. Organic food is grown by both small farms and large organizations.

Answer C is wrong. Organic foods have the same nutrients as conventionally produced food.

Answer D is wrong. There are no universally accepted standards.

Question #50

Answer A is wrong. Conventionally grown food can use pesticides.

Answer B is wrong. They must follow USDA-approved methods for farming that include using only recognized safe fertilizers, pesticides, hormones, and drugs.

Answer C is wrong. The label "natural" has no legal meaning.

Answer D is correct. They must follow USDA-approved methods for farming that include using only recognized safe fertilizers, pesticides, hormones, and drugs.

Nutrition Glossary

Acceptable Macronutrient Distribution Range (AMDR)   Range of intakes for a particular energy source, such as fats, that refers to a reduced risk of disease while providing enough essential nutrients

ACF-certified chef   Member of the American Culinary Federation (ACF) who has completed requirements including a certain number of points earned from education, experience, and rewards, along with culinary work

Acrolein   By-product that occurs when oils are overheated and reach their smoking point, irritating the throat and eyes.

Adequate Intake (AI)   Daily dietary intake level of healthy people that is assumed to be adequate when there is insufficient evidence to set an RDA

Adipose tissue   Body fat

Allergen   Substance that can cause an allergic reaction for some people

Alpha-linolenic acid   Essential fatty acid necessary for normal growth and development

Amine group NH_2 group of atoms in an amino acid

Amino acid   Building blocks of protein

Antibiotic   Medicines that prevent infection

Antibodies   Protein substances that attack unwanted foreign substances in the body and deactivate them

Antioxidant   Chemical that fights the excessive oxidation of molecules in the body

Aspartame   Artificial sweetener made from amino acids that is 200 times sweeter than sugar

Baking   Low-fat cooking method that uses the same techniques as roasting, but for nonmeat items

Barbecuing   Low-fat cooking method in which food is cooked on a grate over indirect heat

Benzoate   Chemical used as a preservative in acidic food items such as fruit juices, syrups, and other items

Beta carotene   Most common precursor or inactive form of Vitamin A that becomes active in the body

Bioengineering   Application of technology to living organisms that produce something of use

Biotechnology   Same as **bioengineering**

Blanch   Boil lightly in advance of need

Body mass index (BMI)   Method of measuring a person's degree of obesity by using weight and height information

Bolus   Ball of chewed food that travels from the mouth to the stomach

Braising   Low-fat cooking method in which meat is seared using the dry-sauté method and then a flavorful liquid containing aromatic vegetables is added to cook the meat

Bran   Outer layer of grain which contains the highest percentage of fiber and nutrients

Broiling   Low-fat cooking method in which food is cooked in a perforated pan over a catch pan with high direct heat from above in a broiler

Carbohydrate   Class of nutrients that includes starches, sugars, and dietary fiber

Carbohydrate loading   Method used by some athletes to maximize the storage of glycogen in their muscles

Carotene   Food additive used by the body to make vitamin A that is used as a yellow food coloring

Center-of-plate concept   Traditional method of plating in which the main element of a meal is focused as an expensive centerpiece item and the rest of the components are accompaniments

Certified organic food product   Product that meets the requirements of a particular certifying entity, such as a government agency or an independent organization

Charque   Another name for jerked beef

Chemical loss   Reduction of nutrients due to destruction or transformation of the chemical composition of food

CHO   Common abbreviation for carbohydrates

Cholesterol   Waxy substance found only in animal food, such as meat, fish, poultry, and cheese

Chylomicron   Digestive lipoprotein that transports triglycerides out of the intestine into the lymphatic system

Chyme   Semiliquid fluid in the stomach made of food that has been partially digested with other fluids in the stomach

Coenzyme   Activators of other enzymes

Collagen   Primary protein of animal and human connective tissue

Colorant   Same as food color

Complementary and alternative medicine   Group of diverse medical and healthcare systems, practices, and products that are not presently considered to be part of conventional medicine

Complementary protein   Food items that, when combined, provide all nine essential amino acids and, therefore, an equally complete protein source

Complete protein   Same as **high-quality protein**

Complex carbohydrate   Those carbohydrates that contain more numerous combinations of saccharides than do simple carbohydrates

Conditionally essential amino acid   Amino acid that may become essential under special circumstances and, therefore, needs to be obtained through food in the same way as essential amino acids

Confit   Process of cooking meat and preserving it in its own fat

Conventional food   Food grown using approved agricultural methods

Coulis   Thick puréed sauce

Crossbreeding   Process of breeding different varieties of plants or animals that exhibit favorable characteristics to yield offspring with the best qualities of each species

Cruciferous vegetables   Broccoli, cauliflower, and cabbage

Culinary arts   Art of preparing food for sensory enjoyment as well as to meet dietary needs

Culture   Way of life within a social group in which there are common customs among members

Daily values (DVs)   Food-label reference values determined from the FDA's Reference Dietary Intakes (RDIs) and Daily Reference Values (DRVs)

DASH   Dietary Approaches to Stop Hypertension; diet that is low in sodium but high in other minerals to help normalize blood pressure

Dehydrating   Reducing the available water by chemically tying it up

Denaturation   Act of a protein structure changing from its naturally folded structure into an unfolded structure

Dental caries   Tooth decay

Dextrose   Natural form of glucose

Diabetes   Disease characterized by high blood-sugar levels (hyperglycemia)

Dietary fiber   Type of carbohydrate containing glucose that cannot be broken down or digested by digestive enzymes

Dietary Guidelines for Americans 2005   Document published jointly by the Department of Health and Human Services and the USDA that offers science-based advice for healthy people over the age of two about food choices to promote health and reduced risks for major chronic diseases

Dietary Reference Intakes (DRIs)   set of daily nutrient and energy intake amounts for healthy people of a particular age range and gender

Digestion   Process of breaking down food to the most simple or elemental parts to be absorbed and used by the body

Digestive system   Hollow tube from the mouth to the anus

Digestive tract   Another term for digestive system

Diglyceride   Molecules formed by one glycerol molecule and two fatty acids

Disaccharide   Molecules consisting of two units (double sugars) of monosaccharide sugar units

Docosahexaenoic acid (DHA)   Polyunsaturated fatty acid that is a so-called "good" fat

Dry-sautéing   Low-fat cooking method in which food is cooked at high heat in a nonstick sauté pan with very little or no oil

Edamame   Same as soybeans

Eicosapentaenoic acid (EPA)   Another polyunsaturated fatty acid that is a so-called "good" fat

Empty-calorie food   Food high in calories, but with few other nutrients

Emulsification   Process in which tiny globules of fat are formed to allow for the complete breakdown of lipid to monoglycerides and free fatty acids that can pass through the small intestine and be absorbed

Emulsifier   Ingredient that enables the formation of water and fat mixtures

Emulsion sauce   Sauce that consists of egg yolk and butter or oil; examples are hollandaise and mayonnaise

Endosperm   Starchy layer that is the largest part of grain and provides flour for white bread and pastries

En papillote   Low-fat cooking method in which food is baked and steamed in a greased paper or parchment bag

Enriched   Process of replacing nutrients that were removed during the processing of whole grain into a refined product

Enzyme   Molecules containing protein that enhance or retard chemical reactions

Essential amino acid   Nine amino acids that cannot be manufactured by the body and must, therefore, be obtained from food

Essential fatty acid   Fatty acid that cannot be produced in the body and, therefore, must be consumed in the diet

Estimated average requirement (EAR)   Estimated average daily dietary intake level to meet the nutritional requirements of half of the healthy people of a particular age range and gender

Estimated energy requirement (EER) Dietary energy intake believed to maintain energy balance in a healthy adult of a certain age, gender, weight, height, and level of activity

Fad Short-term increase or decrease in the popularity of an idea, belief, practice, or product

Fat Lipid that is solid at room temperature

Fat-soluble vitamin Vitamin that is soluble in fat but not in water; can be stored in the body's adipose (fat) tissue

Fatty acid Organic molecule found in animal and vegetable fats that is part of most lipids

Flavor reversion Process in which fat oxidizes before its rancidity becomes apparent

Folate Form of folic acid

Folic acid Water-soluble B vitamin

Food additive Substance or combination of substances present in food as a result of processing, production, or packaging

Food irradiation Treating food with ionizing radiation to reduce or eliminate bacteria and parasites that cause foodborne illness

Food label Label on packaged food that lists the nutrients included and their amounts

Food science Study of changes that occur in food with chemical and physical reactions

Freeze-drying Process of removing all moisture from food to prevent spoilage

Genetically modified organisms (GMOs) Plants or animals whose genetic makeup has been altered

Fructose   Fruit sugar

Galactose   Nutritive sweetener that is less sweet than glucose and not very water soluble

Germ   Small, nutrient-rich inner layer of grain

Glucagon   Hormone that promotes the release and production of glucose by the liver

Glucose   Blood sugar

Glycerol   Three-carbon alcohol that bonds with three fatty acids to produce a single structure

Glycogen   Molecule related to glucose that is used for energy storage in the liver and muscle

Grilling   Low-fat cooking method in which food is cooked on a grate over direct or indirect heat

Gum   Substance that forms a sticky mass in water

Hard water   Water that contains large amounts of minerals such as calcium, magnesium, and sulfur

Harvesting   Process of gathering crops to bring them to market

Healthy   Term that can be used on food labels when certain requirements established by the FDA have been met

Heme iron   Major type of iron in animal food

Hemoglobin   Active molecule in red blood cells

Herbicide   Weed killer

High-density lipoprotein (HDL)   Lipoproteins that transport cholesterol away from body cells

High-quality protein   Food that contains all of the essential amino acids

Home meal replacement   Food that has been made, cooked, chilled, and ready for simple reheating

Hormone   Chemicals containing protein that deliver or carry out important body functions

Hybrid plant   Example of the result of crossbreeding two or more plants

Hydrated   Condition that occurs when the body contains enough water for proper operation

Hydrogenated   Process by which oils are chemically reacted with hydrogen

Hydrolytic rancidity   Process by which oils deteriorate when glycerol separates from fatty acids in a triglyceride

Hyperglycemia   Condition in which blood-sugar levels are high

Hypoglycemia   Condition in which blood-sugar levels are low

Incomplete protein   Food that is missing one or more essential amino acids

Infused oil   Oil that has been heated with seasonings for flavor

In season   Period of time when a food product is harvested

Insoluble fiber   Dietary fiber that does not dissolve in water

Insulin   Hormone secreted by the pancreas that circulates in the blood and helps glucose enter cells to reduce blood-sugar levels

Intermediate-density lipoprotein (IDL)   Lipoprotein that picks up cholesterol, phospholipids, and protein as it carries triglyceride through the blood to the cells

Intrinsic factor   Chemical made in the intestines that facilitates the absorption of Vitamin B_{12}

Iron-deficiency anemia   Disease that occurs when there is a lack of iron in the diet or a problem with absorption of iron in the body that results in low levels of blood hemoglobin

Isoflavone   Chemicals found almost exclusively in legumes and thought to be helpful in reducing cholesterol and cancer

Jerked beef   Meat that has been salted, pressed, and dried

Jus   French term for juice

Ketoacidosis   Life-threatening complication that arises when balance of insulin and blood sugar is not controlled.

Ketone bodies   Completely metabolized products of fatty acid metabolism

Kilocalorie   Energy needed to heat one kilogram (about 2.2 lb) of water by approximately 2°F (1°C)

Kilogram   Equivalent of about 2.2 lb

Kosher   Term relating to Jewish dietary laws

Kwashiorkor   Protein-deficiency disease that occurs when a baby who is supplied adequate amino acids in mother's milk is weaned and then deprived of these amino acids in the subsequent diet

Lactose   Milk sugar

Lacto-ovo-vegetarian   Vegetarian eating pattern that excludes meat, fish, and fowl from the diet

Lacto-vegetarian   Vegetarian eating pattern that excludes meat, fish, fowl, and eggs from the diet

Laxation   Looseness of the bowels

Lecithin   Common phospholipid found in food such as egg yolks, used to hold oil and lemon juice or vinegar in an emulsion

Linoleic acid   Essential fatty acid that is necessary for normal growth and development

Lipid   Class of nutrients that contains triglycerides, cholesterol, and phospholipids

Lipoprotein   Molecules that contain a lipid and a protein

Local produce   Produce grown near the place of its use

Low carbohydrate   Term without legal definition used by marketers to attract consumers to specific food items

Low-density lipoprotein (LDL)   Lipoprotein that transports cholesterol in the blood

Macrobiotic diet   Diet that is similar to a vegetarian diet because the allowed food items are similar, although for different reasons

Macrobiotics   Philosophy of life directed toward improving its quality and length through improved quality of food

Maillard reaction   Browning reaction that results in a particular flavor and color for food that does not contain much sugar, such as roasted meat

Major mineral   Those minerals needed in larger amounts in the body

Maltose   Malt sugar

Mannitol   Sugar alcohol

Marasmus   Protein-deficiency disease that includes muscle wasting and loss of stored fat

Meal replacement product   Liquid drink containing approximately 200 calories that replaces a meal in a calorie-controlled diet

Meat replacement product Product used in vegetarian diets that help vegetarians obtain the needed amount of protein and other nutrients that are found in meat, fish, and fowl

Metabolism Process by which living organisms and cells break down complex chemicals into their components and reassemble them into larger molecules needed by the body

Micronutrient Nutrients including vitamins and minerals that are required in very small amounts in the body

Minerals Inorganic elements that help to regulate the body

Miso Fermented soybean base usually used for seasoning or in soup

Monoglyceride Molecule formed by one glycerol molecule and one fatty acid

Monosaccharide Molecule consisting of a single sugar unit that cannot be digested further

Monosodium glutamate (MSG) Widely used food enhancer

Monounsaturated Fatty-acid molecule comprised of monounsaturated fatty acids

Morbidity Disease rate

Mortality Death rate

Mother sauce Classic sauce from which other sauces are made

Mucosa Mucus membrane of the digestive tract that protects its lining and provides secretions from underlying tissue

MyPyramid Tool developed by the USDA to educate people about balanced diets and the need to include physical activity in their daily lives

Negative nitrogen balance   Situation that occurs when a person excretes more nitrogen than he or she is taking in as protein

Nitrate   Natural constituent of plants that is used in the pickling of meats

Nitrite   Essential agent used in preserving canned meats in the pickling process

Nitrogen balance   Condition that occurs when a person has the same nitrogen intake as nitrogen loss

Nonheme iron   Iron from plant sources

Nutrient dense   Food items that contain large amounts of nutrients and few calories

Nutrients   Chemicals needed to support the body in functions of growth and development

Nutrition   Science of nutrients in food and how they are ingested, digested, absorbed, transported, and used to build and maintain the body

Nutrition Facts panel   Part of the food label that contains the nutrition information required by the FDA

Nutrition Labeling and Education Act of 1990 (NLEA)
Amendment to the Food, Drug, and Cosmetic Act of 1938 that made major changes to the content and scope of the nutrition label and to other elements of food labels

Obese   Term used to interpret body mass index (BMI) that relates to the category of persons who are most overweight

Obesity   Condition of being obese
Oil   Lipid that is liquid at room temperature

Omega-3 fatty acid   Essential fatty acid that is a so-called "good" fat because it is helpful to the body

Omega-6 fatty acid   Essential fatty acid that is a so-called "good" fat because it is helpful to the body

Organic acid group   COOH group in an amino acid

Organic food product   Food product that is assumed to be produced without pesticides or synthetic fertilizers

Oven-frying   Low-fat cooking method in which food is breaded and then baked or broiled at high heat

Overweight   Term used to interpret body mass index (BMI) given to persons with a BMI is greater than "normal" but less than "obese"

Oxidative rancidity   Process that occurs when oils are exposed to air and heat

Pan-steaming   Cooking method in which vegetables are placed in a sauté pan with a small amount of water or stock and then covered and cooked over high heat until the vegetable is tender but not soft

Papillae   Taste buds

Pareve   Food items in a kosher diet that are neither meat nor dairy food

Partially saturated   Fatty-acid molecule that contains more than one double bond

Pastirma   Highly seasoned, dried meat product found today in Turkey, Egypt, and Armenia and that originally came from ancient Greece

Pemmican   Dried meat that has been powdered or shredded and then mixed with fat to form a solid product

Pesticide   Chemicals that kill insects and other plant pests

Phosphate   Chemical used widely within food processing (e.g., leavening agent for baked goods and to tenderize meats)

Phospholipid   Lipid that is part of a cell membrane and links water and fat to form an emulsion

Photosynthesis   Process by which plants store energy

Physical loss   Loss of nutrients due to peeling, trimming, processing, and other physical actions

Phytochemical   Chemical or nutrient derived from a plant; the term is commonly used to refer to chemicals that somehow aid the body in fighting or avoiding diseases

Phytonutrient   Another term for phytochemical

Plaque   Fatty deposits on a wall of blood vessel

Poaching   Low-fat cooking method in which food is cooked gently (just below a simmer) in liquid such as stock, wine, juice, or water

Polysaccharide   Molecule comprised of twenty to thousands of sugar units

Polyunsaturated   Fatty-acid molecule that contains more than one double bond

Positive nitrogen balance   Condition that occurs when there is more nitrogen being taken in than being excreted

Protein   Class of nutrients that provides building blocks in the form of amino acids that are used by the body for building muscles, tissues, enzymes, and hormones and for other purposes

Protein balance   Condition that occurs when a person's protein intake and protein usage are equal

Protein deficiency   Condition that occurs when there is a lack of protein in the diet

Protein energy malnutrition (PEM)   Condition that relates to the deficit of food or an underlying disease that causes a decrease in food consumption from a loss of appetite

Protein turnover   Term that describes how protein is used and then synthesized (combined to form a new product)

Purée   Thick liquid made from finely ground food

Raffinose   Small but complex carbohydrate that, when metabolized, produces intestinal gas

Rancidity   Term that describes fats and oils when they deteriorate and develop an off flavor and bad taste

Recombinant DNA technology   Technology that allows the DNA of an organism to be combined with part of another DNA code, typically from another organism, so that the genetic code of the receiving plant or animal typically is changed

Recommended Dietary Allowance (RDA)   Average daily dietary nutrient intake sufficient to meet the nutrient requirements of nearly all healthy individuals of a particular age and gender group

Reduction sauce   Sauce made by reducing a liquid until it is the consistency of a glaze

Refined   Type of sugar that is extracted from sap and purified

Registered dietetic technician   Member of the American Dietetic Association who has completed an approved two-year undergraduate program

Registered dietitian   Member of the American Dietetic Association who has completed an approved four-year undergraduate program plus advanced training through an internship or master's degree

Resting metabolic rate (RMR)   Amount of energy (number of calories) needed for body functioning at complete rest

Retinol   Another name for Vitamin A

Roasting   Low-fat cooking method in which food is placed on a rack over a catch pan and cooked in the oven

Roux   Cooked mixture of fat and flour

Saccharin   Artificial sweetener that is 300 times sweeter than sugar

Salt pork   Salted flesh of pig

Saturated fatty acid   Fatty acid that cannot accept or bond with additional hydrogen atoms

Seasonal produce   Produce that is locally available only at certain times of the year

Selective breeding   Process that occurs when the best plants of the harvest or the best animals of the herd are selected for reproduction

Shortening effect   Interference with the formation of gluten strands in wheat-based dough that cause it to have a crumbly texture

Side chain   Organic chains or rings of many types of amino acids

Simple carbohydrate   Sugars that are comprised of single carbohydrate units

Slurry   Thin paste made from water or stock that is mixed with starch

Smoke-roasting   Low-fat cooking method also known as pan-smoking

Soft water   Water that contains smaller amounts of minerals than does hard water

Soluble fiber   Dietary fiber that dissolves in water to form a gel that connects to bile salts and reduces cholesterol in the blood

Sorbitol   Sugar alcohol

Sous vide Processing method that involves cooking food in a pouch in a vacuum condition

Soy Legume that is native to eastern Asia but which is now grown throughout the world

Soy milk Product made by grinding dehulled soybeans mixed with water to become a milk-like beverage

Sports diet Combination of higher than normal amounts of protein, sports-diet supplements, electrolyte replacement, and carbohydrate loading, which enhances athletic ability, strength, agility, and endurance

Stabilizer Chemical used to maintain the structure of emulsions

Stachyose Small but complex carbohydrate that, when metabolized, produces intestinal gas

Starch Complex carbohydrate made from combinations of simple carbohydrates (sugars)

Steaming Low-fat cooking method in which food is cooked in a perforated basket over boiling water with no fat

Sterol Hydrocarbons consisting of a steroid and an alcohol and having carbon bonded to carbon in a closed ring (e.g., cholesterol)

Stewing Low-fat cooking method identical to braising except that the meat, vegetables, or fruit are cut into pieces, which are then fully immersed in the flavorful liquid

Stir-frying Low-fat cooking method in which food is cooked over extremely high heat with a small amount of fat in a wok or sauté pan and stirred constantly

Stone ground Grain that is ground into flour with stones rather than modern metal grinders

Sucralose Artificial sweetener that is 600 times sweeter than sugar

Sucrose   Table sugar

Sugar   Most simple carbohydrate

Sweat   Low-fat cooking method in which food items, particularly vegetables, are cooked in a small amount of fat over low heat

Tempeh   Food product made from whole, cooked soybeans that are formed into a cake

Textured soy protein   Product made from soy flour that has been defatted

Textured vegetable protein (TVP)   Another term for **textured soy protein**

Thermic effect of food   Number of calories needed to digest, absorb, transport, and store nutrients in the body

Thickener   Item used to add body to a food product without impacting flavor

Tofu   Bean curd; made from cooked and puréed soybeans

Tolerable Upper Intake Level (UL)   Highest level of daily nutrient intake that poses no risk of adverse health affects to almost all individuals of a certain age range

Trace mineral   Minerals that are needed in smaller amounts than major minerals

Trans fat   Unsaturated fatty acids that act like saturated fats in the body

Transgenic GMOs   Typically, modified food where the DNA of one species is implanted in another

Trend   Long-term increase or decrease in some factor like popularity, weight, a belief or idea, or income level

Triglyceride   Form in which fats are stored in the body

Umami   Savory taste that is experienced all over the tongue

Unsaturated fatty acid   Fatty acid that has at least one or more double bonds in the carbon chain

USDA Organic   Product that is at least 95 percent organic and that meets USDA organic standards

Vegan   Vegetarian who will not eat meat, fish, fowl, eggs, dairy, or other animal products

Vegetarian   Someone who does not eat meat, fish, fowl, or products containing these food items

Very low-density lipoprotein (VLDL)   Lipoproteins made in the liver and intestine that transport triglycerides through the body

Villi   Plural of villus; fingerlike projections in the small intestine that increase the surface area and, therefore, the absorptive ability of the small intestine

Vitamin   Organic compound that helps regulate the body

Water-soluble vitamin   Vitamins that are soluble in water but not in fat, and that are generally not stored in the body

Wheat berry   Whole, unprocessed wheat grain

Whole grain   Grains or food made from grains that contain all the nutritionally essential parts of the grain

Whole wheat   Food-labeling term that indicates the product is made from the whole grain of wheat